S0-CJD-576

The Cocks of Hades

by the same author

*

THE STONES OF TROY

THE COCKS OF HADES

C. A. TRYPANIS

FABER AND FABER
24 Russell Square
London

First published in mcmlviii
by Faber and Faber Limited
24 Russell Square London WC1
Printed in Great Britain
at the Bowering Press Plymouth

To Oswald and Helen

Acknowledgment

The Editors of *The Times Literary Supplement*, *The Spectator*, *Botteghe Oscure*, *The Oxford Magazine*, *Poetry Book Society Supplement*, *Stapledon Magazine*, *Gemini*, *Delta*, *Truth*, *Stand*, *Adam*, *Encounter*, The School of Art, University of Reading, and Third Programme, First Reading, are hereby thanked for permission to reprint some of these poems.

Miracle, bird or golden handiwork,
More miracle than bird or handiwork,
Planted on the star-lit golden bough,
Can like the cocks of Hades crow . . .

W. B. Yeats, Byzantium

Contents

The Pier

The cobbled pier, one more good-bye—
A tall-funnelled ship, the grape-blue sky,
A flutter of hands in the wind,
The harbour-lights stiff with spray,
The heart too stiff to pray,
Void of a burial-mask, blind.

With staring partings, the too many ships,
Too many the rifted and unspeaking lips,
The same cobbled pier, one more good-bye,
A sharp hill's shadow fouling the view,
Fishing-lights burning snares in the blue,
Masts, then funnel, smoke snatched from the eye.

Ships and ships have sailed away,
And I, nailed to that pier watching the grey
Gulls circle, the lights grown stiff with spray—
Or is it always the same painted boat
I saw lift anchor, and my small days float
Down the windy Aegean one August day.

Three Fishermen

Three fishermen, spreading out nets.
All night long they have fished,
The nets are wet, the pier striped with an early sun.
They move bent, fumbling at the ropes,
Eyes, empty strips of light,
Wind-searched faces.
You could not guess their age,
Water is bitterly indifferent.

The fingers move mechanically,
Untangling knots, corks, weeds, slivers of fish.
Sometimes a foot would come to help.
But at another level their eyes are looking.
Is it still the swaying water? A dry room?
Hot food? Some woman's flesh?

Yet, always there, cutting between them
And their view, that cage of nets.
A life full of nets—
To be bought, to be pulled, to be patched,
The round smell of rotting rope
And squashed fish.

The three men reached the end of the pier,
The brown web sprawling on the flag-stones.
Writhing in two baskets their catch,
Sun beating diamonds off the scales.
Over it they stood, light streaming down
Their wrinkled hands.

Having finished their work,
The victims face one another
Across the deadly nets.
A shallow boat beneath the pier
Now softly heaving. . . .

Cock at Sea

The wooden cage was wedged on the ship's prow
Between sails, vomit, chains that groaned all night.
The grey dawn broke, I heard the sick bird crow
Across the bitter water to the light.

The farm was dancing though that jagged cry—
Tall hay-stack, seed-rich field, barn, hedge and tree,
Cocks that could proudly strut, birds that could fly—
And he a captive of the grinding sea.

No answer from that farm, endless the blue,
Endless the waves, the slaps of salty breath.
He crowed again, the day was rising new
To feed this nightmare in the sleep of death.

Chabrias

Such as we are, half mercenaries,
Half idealists, we should remember Chabrias.
He could sting a low, dull spirit
To frenzy, when battle was slanting,
Never sparing his body, his men always.
That is how he broke them to obey,
Go down on one knee, knuckle the shield with the other
And face the scowling Spartans,
Agesilaus.

So Naxos was a steep triumph,
And Athens, the ungrateful, offered him
A golden crown, set up his statue in the
Market-place, accepted his wine for The Mysteries,
Wine of a mercenary of foreign kings!

And most of all we must remember Chabrias,
When we too, abandoned, lie down
To die in the harbour of Chios,
And hear with royal calm, and with no bitterness,
The trampling on the decks, the shouting,
The rush of oars,
As it grows fainter across the water.

The Tragic Mask

The Theban curse, the Atreid's disgrace,
Incest and savaged honour splashed on clay,
A husk of horror, clinging to the face.

The fallen flesh must never try to sway,
Approach the god uncovered. The bronze flare
Of Zeus will turn it to the Furies' prey.

The naked mouth, though crammed with circling prayer,
Can never guide the god to pluck the whips
That arm the barren Daughters of Despair.

Only behind the mask's protective lips
Man can protest, protesting find relief,
The voice that climbs the theatre seats and drips

On gold-pleat friezes—hard gods in relief
Against the burning blue—rolls down the marble eaves,
Mingling with shadows sharper than its grief,

To spread to the clouds and the pale world of leaves.
The world of leaves! From this the autumn wind
Chooses his light-legged chorus as he weaves

Across the empty dancing-floor loop-spined,
To chant the journey of the leaning years.
Maskless the leaves. Is it because they find

That bare or masked the ancient wrongs and fears
Return to wound the ageing flesh tenfold,
That masks can neither hide, nor pay arrears?

Is it they feel the mask a savage mould
Pressing into its shape the stifling heart,
Pressing until it sets—crease, wrinkle, fold?

Masks do not hide, they shape the human heart.

Achaean Queen

Robbers, who knows how many years ago,
Broke through the silence of this tomb,
And stripped the bones of burial-mask and gold.

The gold, a thief of peace, crawled back again
Into the money-making world. Licked by a jeweller's
Flame, it must have flown in other marriage rings,
In other masks of death, linking the men to come
With an Achaean queen. It may be running now
In this my ring, or in the burning cross
Upon the breast of some dark peasant girl.

But in the night, the villagers still say
The soul comes calling to the opened tomb,
To find among the rocks the marble breast
Of its Achaean queen, the arms through which it hugged,
The slanting eyes through which it learnt to laugh.

For this, they say, was a gentle woman's tomb,
One who had known what love and sorrow means.
No haughty king enjoyed this chamber's peace,
No tyrant breaking slaves upon the wheel,
Driving his chariot down the thirsty hill
Among the leaning olives and the vines,
Lips swollen with abuse.

Here slept a gentle woman,
So they say, who knew what love and sorrow means.
And if her mask now hangs a cross upon some praying
Breast, blessed be the thieves. Christ in his mercy
May yet embrace her soul—unchristened fugitive
That drifts across the dark seeking a tomb
Together with the weeping grey-blue owls.

Tithonus

Tithonus, Tithonus, how light
Your hands, like dead white
Leaves at the foot of ancient trees
Under the setting Pleiades.

Tithonus, Tithonus, blue, bird-thin
Your bones pressing the dry skin.
Only Eos' rich young mouth
Could forget to ask for youth.

Sleeping Beauty

He reached the hedge, a wall of curling thorns,
Broke in, and bleeding stared across damp shade
At drifts of ancient leaves, and ancient lawns,
Asleep beneath a marble balustrade.

He struggled on, was forced to kneel, to crouch,
Before he gripped the door, weeds glossed on stone,
Then climbed the marble steps, and on her couch
The Princess slept alone.

Bird-slender throbbed her throat against a rope
Of pearls. This was The Sleeping Beauty, no mistake.
But he was not The Prince, how could he hope?
Why kiss a mouth he could not coax to wake?

Beyond her ogived windows not a thing
Was moving in that garden, still half-cleft
The log lay in the yard—sleep was The King—
And so he turned and left.

And still the garden sleeps, and nothing stirs,
And nobody has found that palace since.
Had he but knelt and laid his lips on hers,
He would have been The Prince.

My Pylades

—'My Pylades, my Pylades'! Is it to Pylades
Orestes speaks?
The grown-up friend? For now those barren beaks
Close in upon a murderer who flees.

Or in this puzzling life of men
Orestes blindly calls on Pylades,
A face belonging to his childhood ease,
Orestes, unhunted Orestes, as he was then?

Tiberius Claudius Rufus

It was not hard for Tiberius Claudius Rufus
'To be decent and to keep the traditional laws
In the presence of the Hellanodikai,
And still to perform acts worthy of the Olympic
Crown, of Zeus, and the true spirit of athletics,'
As the stone decree of the Elians proclaims.
Admittedly, it was not the practice of his times,
When professional wrestler and crush-eared pugilist
Tricked the judges, and duped the cheering crowds,
When the Altis was scarred by the statues
Of fleshy, ape-foreheaded Romans.
But honesty can always be found, and, like health,
Is taken for granted by those who possess it.
Elians of the Empire, only the dishonest
Consider it worthy of particular mention.

The Shipbuilder

Balanced against the skyline
He builds his ship: Saint Nicholas.
A wooden cross on the fresh prow,
Round it a wreath of blazing flowers—
Garlands ringed the prows that sailed
For the Sicilian expedition.
His tools, an axe, a plane, a hammer and a saw,
His eyes, full of the builder's craft
Five generations of boat carpenters had gathered.
On it he stakes all that he has,
Four hundred golden pieces.
For he will sail that ship himself
And trade, and challenge wealth.

Against the straight horizon
He balances the whispering keel,
The swelling flanks, the rearing prow
To cleave into rich orange-blossom
The wine-blue sea, to reach that skyline
So full of white reward.
A puff of cloud? Some fading headland?
Every horizon is a spear to fight brown death.
The paint? It will be red
And green, and gay and full of hope
Like early summer seas.
There is no winter in a builder's heart.
—'Next Spring, the waters blessed,

I will set sail. The wreath of flowers
Will have gone dead, but we shall not wait
For Saint John's to burn it.'
No line is nerved with richer hope than the horizon.

Thera

Blue-capped dome, pink belfry,
Riding the rage of Vulcan,
Snatched in a rush of sky.
Black wounds on a black rock's face,
And the path, forked lightning,
Smoothed by the hooves of mules,
Of donkeys rising slowly
To an arched skyline.
Cupped roofs, watching
The windy Cyclades,
Those mauve anemones adrift
On green-veined water.

Phocaea

. . . they called down mighty curses on whosoever should stay behind. And they sank in the sea a mass of iron, and swore never to return to Phocaea, before the iron should again appear . . . but half the citizens were taken with a longing for the city and sailed back.

Horodotus, I.165

Though you may not suspect it, your Phocaea
Will follow you along the Western coast
To Cyrnus, Marseilles, to dove-rich Elea,
Into long exile sneaks what we love most.

The weakling, the romantic will return,
Breaking his oath, to live a Persian slave.
But you must build rich-speaking cities, turn
Deep Western fields—then, fill a settler's grave.

That iron lump you sank weighs on your heart.
But, were it seen again, were you to steer
Your tall ship fifty-oared back to the start,
You would not find a stone of your Phocaea.

Her temples and her festivals, one frieze
Of virgins stained with amber, gods and men,
Lean only in the eyes of refugees,
That gold-mask all they cannot see again.

Phocaea is dead. She travelled to the heart.
And tell your children that, or else you'll hear—
For they will visit her, if still on the chart—
How ugly and how small they found Phocaea.

The Gordian Knot

And when the sly priest brings you to the knot
That makes men conquerors—a twisting snake
Gripping the yoke to chariot-pole—do not
Slash it with your sword, that's a mistake.
The man who did that conquered, but forgot
He was a man, he stooped to murder, fake
A godly parentage, made his friends plot
Against him. It is no fun to break
The world upon the wheel, and on one hot
Assyrian night to sleep and never wake
Three years and thirty after you were got.
Fondle, then smiling leave the filthy knot.

Death of a Swan

> *Ulanova's mother was also a ballerina . . . as a child Ulanova was made to dance.*
>
> *Bolshoi Ballet Programme*

A flutter of ankles
And wings, points shivering
In lyrical balance.

Honour the virtuoso.
But in those sinews of blossom
Dances the dream of another,
A deep, stifled dream.
It is the self-wasting passion,
The patience, the regret,
Now scourging cruelty
Of another, that feeds
Triumph in The Unique.

Such tragic excellence
Could never have blossomed
Without your frame, Ulanova.
But neither you, without that
Stifled dream, could flutter to death
As any swan would wish to die,
The touch of every dawn
It welcomed on its wings.

Lesbos

Gravel-tormented skull, sharp Sapphic song!
The Pleiades cool on the cheek of dawn,
Foam-legged the wind under a throng
Of gulls, pouring out salty scorn.

And I, between the living and the dead,
Searching a bifurcated beach alone,
Searching the fossil trees and birds that shed
Their spring into the Lesbian stone.

For still, deep in the white-scaled granite block
The forest leans, those leaves an April dyed,
To hear the song that burns across the rock
Of bird-throats petrified.

Voices of spring, by a stone memory stayed,
Sealed in the heart of a headland's cornice,
No agony of death moves in your shade,
No wound, clenched in that paradise.

And yet, the chiselled music fills the light,
The stiffened leaves, the temple of the air,
And on the wind, hymen of that loaded night,
Dances the thistledown that mocks despair.

O tree, carved arms of prayer, trapped in a rain
Of flashing death, stone bird beneath stone leaf,
You wrenched the walls that segment joy and pain
In a still, pastoral relief.

O image, starred beyond the bellied cloud,
Dioscuri to lift the straggling ships,
How soft the rustling, and the song how loud
Behind your speechless lips.

Naxos

Pointed arches open
On climbing white-washed walls,
Flat island roofs, water,
Blue diamond-dust, water, flashing
Crystals of a shrine,
An ancient tyrant's pride.
Look, black-kerchiefed women
Stooping under arms
Of Sanudo and Barozzi, sad
Salt-gnarled eagles,
Crescents, the kissing swords,
Gripped by a marble slab
On crumbling doors,
Where a lost chivalry fights
Decay and the wind.
Not Ariadne, an olive-eyed
Madonna abandoned,
Watches sails
Sink in the wind.
Half-quarried on his back
Stiff Dionysus
Searches a crown of stars.

Village Sisters

The climbing Gothic grey of stone,
A windcock staring on weedy slates,
Green rot, gnarling a gargoyle breast.

The rigid knight who prays alone
Behind locked doors and dim tomb-dates
In a posture not designed for rest.

Your sister of the thirsting South,
In the blue wind a blot of white,
Is opened to goat-herd and goat—full house of god.

And a draggling woman with withered mouth
Mumbles, feeding the oil-fed light
Under ancient saints that bless and nod.

Delphic Afterglow

Ears tuned to a city's noise
Drink in the voice of stillness.
Peak after peak, cool rock,
Sink into one hard skyline
To challenge the Delphic night.
Deep down, green smoke of olives,
Cool haze of silence.
—'First we must learn not to question,
Then to forget anger,
And then that we must not be sad.'
Only a silver spark of sound, a goat-bell.
The land has forgotten her Sacred Wars.
The blistering light is gone,
This is a night of holy stillness.
Was that a cricket calling,
Or silence troubling the deeper calm?

To Theon from his son Theon

(Tubi 18, 2nd century A.D.)

'Theon to his father Theon greetings. Another
Fine thing, father, not to take me to town.
I will not write, or speak, or settle down
Unless you bring me to Alexandria. Mother
Said to Archelaus: 'I can't tell
You how he upsets me. Take him away.'
I beg you, send for me. Until that day
I will not eat, or drink. There now. Farewell'.
This voice, charged with a child's longing, a child's rage,
Called eighteen centuries ago
From the sands where the paper-trees grow.
There is an Alexandria for every age.

The Blind

The hardened eyes will call it a facade,
Realists will call you blind, and blindly rage,
But sightless birds sing sweeter in their cage,
And death comes gentler walking in the shade.

Let's draw the blind, the world behind that screen
Is beautiful, and love no common knave.
The hands that draw the blind are wise and brave,
Those soft dark pleats are proof that we have seen.

Helen

MENELAUS: *She never came to Troy. The gods deceived us. . . .*
MESSENGER: *What did you say? And all that suffering for nothing? For a wisp of cloud?*

Euripides, Helen, 704 ff.

For a wisp of cloud!
That phantom served us well,
Served epic rage.
The steep, grand style,
Rankling in the veins, craves its Troy,
Helen, her ghost, the wind.
How can we keep old Peleus alive,
Unless we kill his son?

Helen, Lydean Helen.
The blood of Zeus darkened her veins,
Forcing a god's aloofness.
Cyprus? The Nile? why not?
But that was no concern of Achilles.
He had to sulk, Patroclus had to die,
And Hector's heel be lashed to that mad chariot.
Paris? Bright ghosts live for the defrauded.
How could we keep old Peleus alive,
Unless we killed his son.

Pogradec

He was young, very young,
A damp patch under the right shoulder—
White asphodels the stars in that deep sky.

Death knows no enemies.
We lifted the fine head, the warmth
Of Tuscany had left so soon.

Only an amulet—a crucifixion—
Behind his fingers' frozen bars.
Taste of the cross in his mouth, and in ours.

The Arrival

He, who had known so much suffering at war and in the painful waves, was sleeping calmly, forgetting . . . they carried Odysseus out first, and put him on the beach sleeping . . . the ship was swiftly moving (on its way back). . . .

Poseidon came near and turned it into a rock, rooting it in the deep.

Odyssey XIII, 90 ff.

Sleep is death-deep, but he can hear the oars
Crushing the foam, beating till he cannot know
Whether his heart is swinging, or the wind that wars
Curled round the grinding prow.

In this soft, healing night
The Laestrygonians and the Cyclopes must seem
The curse on some other man's life, the fight
With angry gods and water moves to a dream.

The moon, dawn-hooded, watched as they laid him down
Sleeping on Ithaca's earth, and from the hold
Pulled out and set beside him brown
Cauldrons, tripods, bronze and gold.

Those who have known long suffering land
Sleeping on Ithaca's shore. They never bend
Over the gunwale to see the home smoke stand
On the sky-line, rejoicing in the journey's end.

He woke, but beyond the olive-grove
There was no Phaeacian ship. He heard the beat
Of oars, or was it his heart? That ship will move
On and on through slanting rain and sleet,

Until it freezes into rock—stone-pale
Hands of sailors clenched on granite oars. They
Are the victims, because Odysseus tricked the god—sail
And stone faces staring through the raging spray.

Kallimachos

He was the monster-killer of Greek knights,
Medusa's head flashed in his red-tongued sword.
Yet he stooped and kissed an Ogress,
Because to kiss her was harder than to kill.

Could her birdless eyes have spoken, told:
'Love will only ransom the princess, and crush the freak?'
But his angered horse reared up, and hurled him deep
Into the withered light beyond the rock.
Yet, as he fell, he had the time to see
A wind of dawn flooding the monster's face,
Her puckered hide melt into royal flesh.

With the day, grape-pickers found him—
Calm eyes, filled with the rolling clouds,
Ribbed bronze, crushing the leaves of grass—
Over him empty the face of the rock.
How could the grape-pickers know
The horror and the dazzle of that kiss?

Prophet Elias Tou Grou

I stand on the rock's brown shoulder,
Where the shallow relief of a saint
Is always blessing the stone-ribbed fields,
The dust of a country road.

Below, sunk in the wind, heavy gateways,
Water-wheels, vine-strangled walls,
Men and bowed women, tufts of dust stumbling home,
Night pressing on the sea.

Gesture of trees, shape of wind the same,
And the stilled voice soft and warm.
Andromeda, Andromeda, which is the flesh
And which the rock?

Now the heart moves out to shrivelled
Hands, claws of migrating birds,
Eyes, the dregs of age, unvisited by broad-winged dreams;
To tortured limbs, blessed only by the stone
Hand of a saint, on whom wind and rain press their mask.

Under the rugged order of the stars,
If you have loved one enough,
Then you have loved them all.

Un Voyage à Cythère

Quelle est cette île triste et noire? C'est Cythère. . . .
Regardez, après tout, c'est une pauvre terre.

Baudelaire, Voyage à Cythère

It lay open on a beach of Cythera
The slender Anthology of English Verse,
Moist in the damp blue dawn.

Silence, not a soul,
And the sand like bloodless lips
Gagged with the kit of soldiers
Who had fled into the brooding night—
Knap-sacks, great-coats, bags, boots . . .

The rock behind the shingle steep enough
To tether the wind, and the village huts empty
Shells, bald eyes gaping at the sea
That jogged along to the far side of the stars.

And the wind, turning the pages of the book,
Blended its voice with the beat of the verse:
'Bring with you all the Nymphes that you can hear
Both of the rivers and the forests greene . . .
Most friendship is feigning, most loving mere folly . . .
Then sing, ye birds, sing, sing a joyous song . . .
When you are old and grey and full of sleep . . .'
The heart of the nation was beating, bare
In the midst of the grand debacle,
'And the bay was white with silent light . . .'

Whose hands had held this paper heart exposed
As the thunder-clouds growled from the North?
Whose unlucky manhood, caught in a world of flame
Had been eased by the graceful book?
And is the blood quickened by those lines
Still flowing? The mind still bruised with the picture
Of the cruel Cytherean beach?

Your paper heart, my unknown friend,
I picked up and carried away with my ship,
My thoughts like sea-gulls circling
Round the ropes of the dipping mast.

Cnossus

Minoan ships are sleeping in the trees,
The tight-hipped men, frieze over stucco frieze,
With blue-scaled fish that swallow and exude
An ochre sea, bulls in steep solitude.

At the King's festival—red petals blown
Across a wide court's emptiness,
How silent the libations of distress,
And soft the brush of wrinkled feet on stone . . .

All round, the climbing waste of broom,
The flower-cups swollen with the royal gold,
The buried jars that niggardly hold
Their hollow gloom.

King Minos' justice! feather-tilted scales
To weigh the thistledown that swirling sails
Out through the night, where neither tears nor gold
Can bribe the brooding gods when all is told.

The Half-Wit

D.B.

They landed him with debts, fatigues, disgrace,
The half-wit smiled and brooded, smiled again.
And still they jibed and threw into his face
Rough jokes that petered out in half-wit pain.

Yet, he would always help, would be the first
To shoulder any dead-beat soldier's pack,
Climbing Albanian hills in frozen thirst,
Till death, a rough joke, slapped him on the back.

And there we let the gaping half-wit lie,
No more a soldier's laughing-stock, stone blinds
Hiding his island love, the windy sea.

Albanian rocks above him scratch the sky,
His limping thoughts, spaces between the winds,
His heart, sunk in the wrinkles of a tree.

Sleep

Softly, on tip-toe let us creep
Where slanting eyes unlearn to weep,
Back to the garden shoulder-deep
In gold chrysanthemums of sleep.

Even the pilgrim heart obeys
The call of long Aegean days,
Where nonchalance adrift still lays
Upon those eyes a golden haze.

There, winds of healing midnight blow,
Come let us wander, let us go
Back to the garden, where still grow
The gold chrysanthemums that know

How to unruffle, how to keep
Sorrows sleeping, let us creep,
And wander once more shoulder-deep
In gold chrysanthemums of sleep.

Tsamikos

At first he sat brooding over his drink
In the hunched sea-café,
A sailor at war with the world,
Outcast of love and the fields.
There was nothing young about his face,
Though he was under thirty.

Then, he muttered something to his wine—
When life presses hard, we turn to words,
And ugly words are the most precious.
After, he began to hum low, plaintive
Drifts of a song, like the wind and the rain
That had searched so sharply his face.

Suddenly, lost in a corner, a man
Plucked the strings of a squat guitar.
Also fully alone, he went to meet a remorseless tune,
Rich whippings of sound, bright
Like sunlight on fish-scales
In a good morning's haul.

The sailor rose silent, staring at nothing,
Then started circling in a lonely trance,
His eyes, his limbs, his entire frame
Dripping a bitter, dry complaint—
Tsamikos, the dance of man abandoned.
When words and song fall short
Then only dance can speak,
And suffering can ride a sun-gay tune.

But the dancer and the player never met,
Each circled alone in his own tense world.
Slowly the sailor moved
In rounds lonely and inescapable
As the men's lives on the sea,
Always the same, and somehow always new,
His limbs flecked like a bow,
Like the horn of the waves, his eyes.

Man betrayed was dancing to himself,
And the pulse of his throat, the stroke
Of the squat guitar, the swing of the waves
Were one. The long iniquity of life
Had beaten him back into himself,
And dance, the healer, had handed out
A new defiant slant on love and water,
The gods now his dancing dolls.
For dance can lead you out
Of the inflexible, lonely corner,
As the tragic chorus knew.

Only two pictures on the walls,
Two fly-blown prints, were looking on:
Rich-bosomed Genovefa, sprawling on a luscious couch,
And black Othello, scowling at his sword.
Would that sword have dropped blood,
Had Othello learnt to dance?

The Painted Bird

A girl, carved on the lid of stone,
No name, no single word,
But on the tomb's shoulder alone
A painted bird.

Her body smooth once, burning white,
Now loosely heaped, time-blurred,
But still the heart speaks to the light,
A blue-winged bird.

Looks at the slanting winter storm—
She looked but never stirred—
Waits for the April sun to warm
A painted bird.

The feathered singers filled the air
With songs she never heard,
So far away, though poised so near,
The blue-winged bird.

With open beak, about to sing
And greet the Etruscan day,
A painted bird, just taking wing,
That will not fly away.

Pheidippides

Some goat-bells up the grey Arcadian hills,
A pipe. Hooved Pan, perhaps? the wind?
The swollen lung, the fire-veined ankle kills,
But still more road ahead than left behind.

And then, brash, bigoted Sparta, at the cost
Of such an effort, not to stir a jot!
The Marathons are always won or lost
Whether Pheidippides runs fast, or not.

Bronze Tears

Across the face of bronze one jagged tear.
Can figures of green metal, limbs of stone,
Pentathlon victor and charioteer,
Have hearts that melt in water when alone?

What shadow could have moved in those hard veins,
What memories to soften eyes of bone?
The young athletic bronze never complains,
It must be I, who weep to-day alone.

But no. Against the cool shell of the sky
That sucked the Delphic rock's autumnal flame
I wiped the bronze cheek of a statue dry,
The drops were drops of fire, my fingers lame.

Cicada

Grey, dry-ribbed singer of the summer heat,
Sharp wrinkled wings and legs clawed on a bough,
You voice the naked beauty of the noon.
The yellow warmth, wading across the wheat,
Tramples on clotted scars of fork and plough;
The grass leans on his spear for breath, and strewn
Lie sheaves and scythes and limbs, when burning white
The birdless midday finds your cry to stun
Man with a hammer sharper than the light
Under the pointed arches of the sun.

No breath of wind to swing the bearded thorns,
The wine-press dry, sun-gagged the olives choke,
Under loose walls the drag-tail lizard hides,
The goats packed in the lean splashed shade, their horns
Tripods of twisted bronze in dazzling smoke,
A rusty dust-haze throbbing round their sides.
The wind-mill on the beach stupefied, still,
Sand cutting water like a burning knife,
But for your song that swells beyond the hill
Pan's holy silence would have smothered life.

Royal Tomb

Under a golden mask the tall king lies,
Slaves, dogs, beyond his feet, charred in a hole.
The flame, gripping to ash face, shoulders, thighs,
Will never touch the soul.

Tall kings must rule and tight-hipped slaves must serve,
Whether in blue-friezed palace or dark tomb.
So privileged that royal flesh and nerve
Blossoming from a sacred womb.

Over them, standing steep, the burial mound
Faces the orchard-blotted, wide estates,
Deep streaks of cypresses, burts of palm round
Cyclop walls and griffin-mounted gates.

What cries, what prayers, what armies North and South
That day the blue anemone of death
Curled round the king's eyelids and rich-lipped mouth
To stifle in his throat the imperious breath!

Who knows? Who cares? Yet, here the faithful slave,
Burnt, buried with the dogs in a black hole,
Touched greatness, what the gods expected, gave,
And so fulfilled the nature of his soul.

Such perfect slaves glide through the bronze gate
Of Death proud as any king! In Hell
And Heaven degree must wither, and the great
Are the fulfilled—their king has served them well.

Silence

Slacken the straining ear,
The song struck from the bell,
Close dancing diamond clear,
Has floated away with the swell

To the reeds and the shells of the bay,
To the net-webbed boats behind
The pier, has withered away
In the grooves of the Western wind.

The latticed winter leaves
Shivered, and then sulked still,
The stacks that swallowed the sheaves
Drank music, climbing the hill

To the windy chapel, the saint
Blessing his rock-ribbed fields,
To the drifts of sky that paint
Blazons on cloud-white shields.

Stillness now smooth-footed sneaks,
Yet this hush has a tongue, is a part
Of the anxious silence that speaks
Between the knocks of the heart.

My Love

My love stands honeydusted in a frieze
A yard or two above the temple's door,
Her dress soft-pleated in the marble breeze.

And I below, a foot-fall on the floor
Drifting to join the wisps of ancient prayer—
My only hope to hunger more and more.

Beyond the rock her arrested eyelids stare
At spring and autumn leaves, trapped in stone calm,
The same that numbs her limbs, though shaped to dare

The outburst of sharp love—across them warm
And light-legged shadows linger, wind
Round, narrow thigh and pitcher-lifting arm.

And I, the dust below, head tilted, blind,
A cave-born bat that struck against the sun—
Long hours, tied to tall pillars and the wind.

Eurydice

Orpheus, raging Orpheus,
Plucking the vivid strings
To bring Eurydice back to the light,
Did you not hear the struggling shadows cry:
—'My hand, my toe, my hair, my eye!'
Was not the wind that touched her bending
Head, full of the voices of corrupted night,
Sighs of the bodies you had robbed?

She moved away alone.
But if all Hades' shadows hardened into flesh,
Would not broad Heracles grip half an arm,
The other split in fifty hanks of cowards?
Bright Helen sob with splintered face,
Her moon-soft cheeks now patched
In fifty untoothed hags?

Orpheus, when you plucked the raging lyre
That forced the tears in Charon's horn-hard eyes,
Did you not hear the shifting leaves,
The bumbling stones, the creaking veins of ore?
They all had something of Eurydice to give,
They danced, as she, sucking the honey
Of your lyre, followed you step by step.

The pool of thumb and neck and thigh
And rock and leaf! Yet one is Hamlet's
Mask, Orestes' is another.

The voice that curls those patchwork lips,
Hard, soft, afraid, speaks only once
And brings—don't lose a word—
News to the living from the dead.

The Constant Tin Soldier

One of the little boys took the lame soldier and threw him into the stove . . . no doubt the Black Conjurer must have had a hand in it. . . . The next day the maid found his remains in the shape of a little tin heart.

Hans Andersen,
The Constant Tin Soldier

When all in gold and scarlet march to fame,
And only you—they happened to forget,
Or had run out of tin—are trudging lame,
The last man in the set;

When twelve beats, and each fingered toy
Leaps up to live, to joke, to sing, to dance,
And only you, a stranger to that joy,
Behind the pleated curtains glance

At a slender Ballerina whirling white
Like thistledown across the mellow sky,
Don't let the heart be choked by that midnight,
Don't blame the Conjurer's dark scowling eye.

There is no Conjurer, there is no blame.
Life is the same
For all, the able and the lame:
A little heart of tin caught in a world of flame.

Pentheus

Snatch dappled skins, ivy to cap the head!
Sharp manic flutes, the satyr's phallic leap,
Raw flesh to shred in swelling Bacchic rage!
I see wild Agave, eyes whirling red,
Clutching the draggled head of Crassus, sweep
Across the marble stage!

Shatter the strict frame, smash through your cage,
Throw to the wind black streaks of tangled hair!
A frenzied darkness, tattered by the whim
Of trailing torches—no light, no law, no age!
Tear,
Tear into leather tails the shield's bronze rim!

Tear, till the staggering eyes can see no more,
And turn to hate the bellied Bacchic storm.
Until the gods of light take pity, call
The twisted flesh from mid-sea to the shore.
Slaves of the unpredictable, freedom is form,
And tall, free death the purest form of all.

The Rag Doll Blueleyla

Blue splashed ink lashes
And blotted eyes
Can spread through the blood,
And cling to the marrow.
With the hardness of children
Wrecking what they prize,
We buried her laughing
By the grave of a sparrow.

They dug up that garden
Year after year.
Spade and fork,
The rake and the barrow
Made havoc of all
That was haunted and dear—
The rag doll, red tulips,
Carnations the sparrow.

And our hearts were dug up again
Year after year,
Rooted out, torn,
Then patched and made narrow.
But room has been left
For a ripening tear:
The grave of a doll,
The wings of a sparrow.

Why Did I Choose That Man

At some stage in our life we pick up our younger self dead off the battlefield.

W. Bethe

If we could meet our younger self, we would hardly recognize him.

K. Palamas

Why did I choose that man among the dead,
So many heaped bronze-shirted on the ground,
Blood streaking down their armour poppy-red,
Ravenous dogs and vultures circling round?

Could I have met them long before? Those eyes,
That cheek, nudging the helmet's harsh bronze cheek?
Or was it through his marble sleep's disguise
Those lips, half-parted in the struggle to speak,

Muttered some secret of our earlier days—
The boy that laughing takes to the blind track,
The morning smoke unfolding through the haze
That neither words nor hands can gather back?

I heaved him into the chariot, drove away
Across the plain towards the Achaean camp.
Like trailing stars, handed from night to day,
The horses galloped down the windy ramp.

And, as I drove, I gazed down at the dead,
Jogging against the livid sky of Troy.
A broken tulip lolled his boyish head—
Myself perhaps, when half a man, half boy?

Through dust and wind how could I recognize?
And then for what? No healer now, no priest
Can coax away the sleep that drowns his eyes,
All I can give him is a burial feast.

A feast, where the Achaeans will say good-bye,
Bronze, wet with tears, and torches sadly flash,
Until on his tall pyre against the sky
The long flames lick the body into ash.

The Angels' Castle

Castle of the Angels, a scatter of stones,
Some only clinging to their edges,
An ancient eagle's wind-blanched bones
Piled where salt gnarls the ledges.

Autumn strikes honey from the cypress cones,
The clouds hang loaded, all the light is dead.
Deep down the shingle on the beaches groans,
The water's fringe, a line of melting lead.

No feel of flesh upon this rock, wind-scarred
The limpet of a chapel clinging there—
Walls vaulted, portal cracked and double-barred
Against weather and prayer.

And we, searching for the Angels, crossing doors
Of sullen wind—no sign of guard or porter.
Nobody there, the slapping of their oars
Sucked in the timeless talk of water.

Poppy-black, a moon on either wing,
A butterfly among the fanged stones!
An Angel's soul, coming to bring
Some message to the castle's random bones?

How long, then, must the soul some windy day
Grope for the home she knew, touching a while
Her toys and fantasies of broken clay,
Searching the eyes through which she learnt to smile?

Or is the horror loosened in the flesh so deep,
That on those moonlit wings no soul lies curled—
Blind peelings of some Angels' flesh that creep
In travesty to touch their broken world?

Where are those lucky grains of dust,
Those star-sucked morsels that escape,
Are never churned through mind, nor must
Go through soft Hell of flesh in human shape?

To be some such unruffled, dancing grain,
Out of the grip of memory that mocks
At love, a pearl of froth the tall storms strain
Against those barren rocks!

Leuconia

THE DROWNED CITY

A

—'Do not remember me young. Remember me,
When the stone was no longer smooth,
When the damp flow of time
Had stamped green stillness
On my temples, my streets.
There were no more homecomings,
My trees, the skeletons of ancient hands.
The young must learn memory.'

Onlooker

That voice came from the sea.
Like a cool skull, lulled by green water,
The shell of a drowned city.
Thin the white sunlight
On the face of that deep water.

B

Homecoming

Young Sailor

—'Take them, take them, my silver, my gifts,
All that the bruised brown flesh of a seaman can bring,
But not the heart.'

Old Woman

—'Welcome home, my child, welcome home.'

Young Sailor

—'Strange, but that heart is neither here, nor away!
Why did you curse me with such a heart?'

Old Woman

—'Welcome home, my son, welcome home.'

Young Sailor

—'I know little about eyes,
But there is limited space in the eyes,
And travelling fills that space.
They are awkward, revengeful things.
Eyes may be sunk in the landscape,
And yet be truly looking backwards
Into the head, groping for ripening images.
When you have been away long years,
Your eyes are full. There is no room left
For the changes at home.
It is only the old things they see.'

Old Woman

—'Welcome home, my son, welcome home.'

Young Sailor

—'Home? Home is a point of view,
Eyes tuned to a certain length of light.
When you no longer look at the world
From a window of your island house,
When every bellied boat tacking away
Does not carry your heart in the rigging,
Then you no longer have a home.
House, wind-ripened walls, wistaria,
The grave of the doll and the robin,
Stop growing old. They freeze into a standstill
And stare ten or thirty years ago—
To remember is not to belong.'

Old Woman

—'Welcome home, my son, welcome home.'

Onlooker

Death is a sort of homecoming—
And that is why I am afraid of death.
We expect too much from homecoming.

Old Woman

—'Welcome home, my son, welcome home.'

Onlooker

Have you noticed how great plays
Live on in the shell of a theatre?
How Hamlet, or Lear, or Oedipus,
Though acted long ago,
Leave the gesture of suffering
In the grain of wood and stone,
In the paint of the empty stage?
It is the same with houses.
Happiness and suffering of the flesh
Glows in their flaking shells,
And if the son, the husband, the old father,
Hamlet, or Oedipus, or Lear,
Are played out with a self-consuming passion,
They turn the stone into a beating heart.

Young Sailor

—'What do I see? A statue carved in the rock?'

Onlooker

A young girl in the arms of the ravishing wind,
Tensed against the stone. Under, the endless blue.

Young Girl

—'And the wild sea-monster. . . .'

Onlooker

A pot-bellied captain, squat-set fifties,
Nose full of pox . . .

Young Girl

—'Perseus, Perseus,
Take me away . . . your wife, your servant,
Your slave. . . .'
—'Your slave, your servant. . . .
Your slave. . . .
Slave. . . .'

Onlooker

And the brusque eaves of the rock
Once more thick with silence,
Where the black legs of gulls go wading.

Young Girl

—'Perseus, Perseus,
Take me away . . . your wife, your servant,
Your slave . . .'
—'Your slave . . .
Slave . . .'

Onlooker

There is no Perseus, only the match-maker,
Soul-monger, seller of flesh.

Everything is full of sea.
The eyes, the bones, the skin,
The gnarled door-step—the round smell
Of damp wood and rotting nets.

Young Girl

—'No Perseus . . . no Perseus . . .'

Onlooker

There is no Perseus.

Young Girl

—'Watch when the day is white,
Watch when the sea birds flock,
Chased by the black-legged night—
Which is the flesh, which the rock?

Wait say the wind and the sea,
Wait for the sailor to reach
The time when his ship turns back to a tree,
The bridge translated, a hut on the beach.

Stitch and embroider the rose
On arms hoisting long sails,
The curling Triton blows
At red-scaled mermaid tails.

Wait till the sails are his own,
And his pouch and haunches spread,
Till the island wind has blown
The dream from the dreamer's head.

Wait? How long? Can one tell?
Too soon the 'long' grows 'longer'.
Wait. Your father will sell
Your flesh to the old soul-monger,

You will fall into her dry hands,
That soften only when they hold
The one thing she understands,
An old man's gold.

The wind-bitten doorstep, the rock,
The sea's womb breeds hard-skinned men.
Young sailors do not come to dock,
But melt in the long wind again.

Remember the shy-smiling bride,
Brought to her new mother's home,
The white pleats of her peplos hide
Eyes that roam

Towards the hard sky-line. Try to believe
In the wisdom of the crowd—
Those gold-blood flowers you weave
Grew on Penelope's shroud.

Sit on the door-step, watch white
Day melt away, the seagulls flock
To hide from black-legged night—
Which is the flesh, which the rock'?

Onlooker
A huddle of men, staring into their wine-cups,
Listen. The sailor speaks:

Young Sailor

—'The sea has her own justice.[1]
Not like the land full of words and delay.
Wind, wave and windrift all travel fast,
And the sea's retribution,
For what is done at sea is soon forgotten.
The sea is without memory.
We left Olvia at morning;
The sky's foundations floated white,
The sun was white, dirty, an unwashed sail.
Dolphins nosed for the wind,
The sea-gulls dragged in their necks,
Looking for landfall.
But there was trouble in the town,
We had to leave. All day we sailed,
But then the wind changed round.
—'Down with the sails', shouted the captain,
Old Cleon.—'Not a stitch on the mast'!
Night was falling like a black winding-sheet.
Poseidon, how it came! South-East,
The worst of the Black Sea.
Lost is the grain of corn
That falls under the millstone!
All night long he beat us.
We heard the keel whisper, speak under us, shriek,
We felt it shiver like a reed's leaf.
For every wave that left the ship

[1] The young sailor's story is a version in verse of a Modern Greek story to be found in A. Karkavitsas' *Logia Tes Proras*. I include it here to show the continuity of life in the Aegean.

Two more came on. Our hands were frozen hard—
They are flesh, you see, not bronze—
And then dawn broke. Better it had never come!
White smoke, green smoke, tufts of froth
Whirled into the heaving sky.
The jerking mast was ripping clouds and froth.
Then, worse than fear and cold, hunger set in,
Our food snatched by the sea. Wind our helmsman,
We fell under the mountains of Tauris,
Cold flash of snow against the bitter sky.
Then one of us called out: 'A sail, a sail!
Starboard, a sail'! Half-dazed I called out too:
'A sail!', though I saw nothing, nothing.
We waved weakly with draggled flags,
Praying to the angry god, then saw it
A ship, mastering the sea. I saw captain,
Coxswain and all her crew, all staring at us—,
They came so near—I even read her name:
Soter, the Saviour. We cheered, but they stared on
Without gesture, without recognition,
Then sliding by our stern, passed clean away.
—'The god-damned bastards!', Captain Cleon shouted.
—'Help, help us, we are sinking . . . can't you see. . . .
Save us brothers. . . .'
A dim voice answered: 'Yes, in some future life.'
A cloud of curses followed that ship's wake.
I fell back on the deck—then it was night.
I cannot tell how long I slept,
But remember being woken up by men
Hauling off wet clothing and wet skin.

That was another boat. The sea was flat,
Hills East and West, snow flashing in the sun:
The Hellespont, and we bound for Piraeus,
Our first port holy Delos;
Her grey low harbour, under the holy houses,
Good for Eastern winds. But when it turns to North
You leave, or else you sink.
Thirty boats lay in the anchorage,
A big slave-market and a shrine, you see.
No sooner had we moored, than old Captain Cleon
Began raving like a bag of demons,
His bulging mouth vomiting sailor's oaths
In every tongue:—'The dirty shit-dog,
Filthy shepherd, god-damned undertaker, I'll show him'. . .
For almost nudging our bows,
Who should be anchored, but *The Saviour*!
God, what a fight to hold him back—
You must not fight on holy Delos.
He muttered and he spat:—'The sea, the sea,
She will speak soon! The sea will pay!'
The sun dropped like a withered rose
Beyond the hills of Syros,
The sky's grey skirting-board grew black,
The lowlands white as chalk,
Teno's quick headland pulled on a black mask.
Then everyone ran to the sails, lugged at the oars,
And made for sea—ropes, anchors, nails, teeth at work.
The enemy slanted down at us. The Thracian wind
Came whipping the black snow-storm.
The harbour—no more ships,

Wood, metal, flesh, everything swimming,
Everything screaming.
At dawn the sight was death: rigging afloat
Among the shredded ships and drowned flesh.
And there, before our eyes, the flanks
Of *The Saviour*, the name floating, there,
Among the jogging flotsam!
The sea had passed its judgement.
It took less than a week.
Its justice like its wind and spray
Quick, because it has no memory.
The sea cannot bother to remember.'

C

First Chorus Song

The Chorus of the Winds

North:

Fear me when I am young. Waves swelling
Like the unripe breasts of the Virgin,
Keels clinging to loosening ships.
Set sail when I am old, when the clouds hang
Heavy benevolent eyebrows over wrinkled eyes,
Eyes that have seen too much to be angry.

South:

I am the evil here. Catch me young
And escape, but terror rears in my age.
The horn of my water cuts free

Like beaten sand. The bellies of my waves
Burst full of striking vipers.
Because of me the anchorage is blessed.

East:

Slow, slanting drizzle,
Wet sails, wet oars, wet ropes, wet wood.
Pray, for you can neither sail, nor sing, nor drink.
Behind dim windows, the eyes are watching
At rivers dragging far into the sea
A yellow band of silt.

West:

I side-beat the water till it swerves,
And like a hunted swallow flash a grey-white belly.
Sea-weed, iodine shadow, blots the beach.
Hair trailing in water, soft limbs
Half-sucked in the long-toothed fury,
Hopes of homing ships.

Dead Calm:

And then the white pause, day of the halcyon.
Blanch light, islands sailing off the sea.
Rocks, headlands, wind-scratched roofs
Under a bunch of blue triumphant grapes.
Sails in the sun, wind-weary hands,
The hearts wind-wearied in rest.

D

The Five Doorways

(i)

Child in Love

Onlooker

And here a child in love
Poised under a dark doorway,
Deep in a green dream;
The one foot raised gently, the eyes tensed,
Drowned in wonder, horn light,
Winding between shadows, love and death.

Rich in silence that early
Contemplation of simple beauty,
The pulse rippling on the sunburnt throat,
But the lips closed.
And in the tilt of the head
No adolescent insolence.
A world of no words,
You cannot enter the dream.

(ii)

Mr. Euphorion

Onlooker

Under the next doorway a man stands
Muttering:

Schoolmaster
'"A speaker of words and a doer of deeds",
But you must be especially a speaker of words.
Only then you know how to think,
And only then you can act.'

Onlooker
Mr Euphorion, the school-master, middle-aged,
The man trapped in the mystery of words.
He took everything in the reverse order.
A pupil of Apollodorus, who was a pupil
Of a pupil of Isocrates,
Isocrates, master of words!
It is not easy to be brought up
In the great tradition of words.
Words, words, powerful words,
Beautiful words, words chasing
After their tails, flea-bitten dogs.

And a teacher of words
Can suck the brains out of a skull,
As fully as those brats on the pier
Suck the slimy life out of the sea-urchins—
Then, throw the prickly shell back into the water.

Schoolmaster
—'If you can master words, then you can master
The sea; you do not need her for a living.'

Boy

—'Yes, Sir.'

Onlooker

That was the voice of a small snotty boy,
Who ran ripping his sides with laughter
At the first corner of the street.
You must be out of sight, of course,
To laugh at Mr. Euphorion.

Schoolmaster

—'Here, at this back of nowhere, nobody
Understands me. Isolation, isolation,
The fate of all great men. Athens, of course. . . .'

Onlooker

A curiosity of tiny gold-scaled fishes
Threaded the water. Their mouths gaped
And closed; bubbles climbed to the surface,
Alpha, beta, alpha, beta.
'I weep for Diotimus, teaching small boys
Alpha, beta. . . .' If it were Athens, of course. . . .

Schoolmaster

—'"It missed Patroclus, but struck Pedasus,
The mortal horse, who shrieked his life away"—
Certain grammarians condemn Homer
For putting a mortal horse in the side-traces
Of a chariot, pulled by immortal horses.
They fail to see the point. The poet wishes
To demonstrate the nature of his hero,
Which was partly mortal and partly divine. . . .'
—Alpha, beta, alpha, beta, alpha, beta. . . .

'On the other hand the much-praised line:
'How like the generations of the leaves
Are the generations of men' is, strictly speaking, wrong.
Men live longer than leaves,
And leaves can neither read nor write.'
—Alpha, beta, alpha, beta. . . .

Onlooker

Three naked boys dived off the bowsprit
Of an anchored caique. They were diving after a penny.
The coin flashed silently down the steep water.
The one swooped swiftly up, the penny burning
Between his teeth.
How close he must have come to the sunken cemetery,
To the grave of Mr. Euphorion, where his empty skull
Still clenches between his teeth a small silver coin!
He had talked his way into Hades,
But could he talk his way out again?

The other boys bobbed on the water
Cursing. The curse was grammatically wrong.
Poor Mr. Euphorion! Still, they were laughing,
The world owed them nothing,
Because they did not know how to use words correctly.

Alpha, beta, circled the sea. Lost in the ooze
Mr. Euphorion's fingers
Wrapped round the shadow of a cane.

(iii)

The Veteran of the Melian Expedition

Onlooker

Another voice broke in:

Veteran

—'Do you know what it means
To have believed all your life in the Athenians,
And then to be treated like dirt?
Justice holds good only between men
Of equal power.'

Onlooker

A veteran of the Melian Expedition,
Seated on a doorstep, picking at the root
Of a broken tooth—by now he had only roots—
Staring into darkness.
(Old age is old age, only where there are no
Spectacles and no false teeth).

Veteran

—'They made us fight like dogs,
Killed our men, and then asked for higher taxes!
The Greek cause! Athenian culture—to Hell with that!
But always, since I was a boy, it was Athens.
Athenian manners, Athenian clothes,
Athenian culture. They nourished my childhood,
They fired my manly spirit! Yes, it was a blow
To find that only in my own eyes was I an Athenian.
To them—just one more foreigner, an ally, a Colonial.
Outside Athens, there is no Athens.

But it was good fighting with the Athenians. . . .
On the decks Attic oars, Attic sails,
In the field Attic shields, Attic spears,
The Attic tongue, the Attic turn of mind!

And when that rage of joy was over—
The screaming and the trampling on the decks,
The slapping of the oars—
Even lying wounded in the depth of the ship—
Poseidon, how rough it was!—and what satisfaction
To be wounded among Athenians. A shock, of course,
To hear what they had done, how they had treated
The Melians, and that only the beginning.
Again and again they made us feel like dirt.
Time came, when they did not even stop
To pick up their own dead and wounded.
But such is life. Even Athenians have their faults,
Great faults.

Wars and wars. They come, they go. Some die, some return.
The crippled are the worst.
You would have thought people would honour
And remember them, because they fought.
All that the normal man desires is to forget them.
They are part of the war, and wars must be forgotten.

Yes, the Athenians. They were not
What I had thought. But if a war should come
My way again, I would fight it with the Athenians.
Yes, I would fight with the Athenians again.
I may not be a part of Athens,
But Athens is a part of me. Too late to change.'

(iv)

The Praying Prostitutes

Onlooker

Then came a body of voices:

—'I will raise this voice to the Lydian reed.
Garlanded, I will sing to the pure,
The goddess of deep forests,
Of sun-sharp mountain-tops. . . .'

Onlooker

Some were young, some heavier, older,
But the eyes and limbs of the girls
Glowed round the altar.

—'You who follow the freckled deer,
Purest of all that is pure . . .'

Onlooker

In the courtyard women were praying,
Their slaves kneeling with them,
Right shoulder free to the sun,
The white stone of the wall, like sunburnt salt,
Thwarting the morning wind;
Repeating mechanically
Words half-understood,
Eyes subdued by a distant light,
At a girl's initiation,
Fragile and sad in her purity.

Under the lintel of the door
Three draped women watching. Prostitutes.
They had somehow drifted in. Curiosity?
A mistake? They watched, but never moved,
True to their own rules of right and wrong.

But here in this courtyard
This quiet morning, something has been changed.
They keep their faces secret.
A square foot of cloth
Can cover worlds of abandon.

The girl knelt, lifting a cup to the flames.
The prostitutes fumbled for some word of prayer,
Some childhood memory. Any prayer would do,
One phrase, one word—

—'Pure maiden of the hills. . . . Pure maiden of the hills . . .'

To cover dry sobbing.
A prostitute's soul on holiday
Can have its own purity—

—'Pure maiden of the hills. . . . Pure maiden of the hills . . .'

The intense purity of the impossible,
Pride in ashes.

—'Pure maiden of the hills. . . . Pure maiden of the hills . . .'

And no spark can excite
The white heart of Artemis more,
Than the rare flame struck
From the rock of sin.

—'Pure maiden of the hills. . . . Pure maiden of the hills . . .'

Gladly the goddess received her. . . .

(v)

The Old Hag

Onlooker

Then other voices, confused, refracted:
—'Stop, you fool. The child is your wife's . . .'
—'Murder?'—'Yes, since she is a party to it all . . .'
—'Where are you going? Where are you off to . . .'
—'Glycera, give in, forgive him . . .'
—'Give me the box with my sewing . . .'
—'My brother got his share, of course . . .'
—'Share of course . . .
Of course . . .'
Till at the end of town
Floated the old Hag's hut.

—'My magic wheel, bring to my house the man I love . . .'

An old hunched woman in a black shawl,
At day-time alone, but not after dark.
Children are warned: 'Never go near
That doorstep, she has The Evil Eye.'

—'Circe, Medea, and golden-haired Perimede . . .'

But this old hag can bring back the lover,
The straying husband, can find what has been lost,
Can bring down a curse on the right head—
She has even spoken with the dead!

Scarred yellow fingers are mixing flour
With herbs and milk from the breasts of mother
And daughter. She is kneading a donkey's brain,
Muttering an incantation—'Turn, turn, turn . . .'

After so many years, the old witch herself
Almost believes in her art.
But deep in the sockets of her red eyes
Clings a flash of that surprise
The first time her magic worked.

—'My magic wheel, bring to my house the one I love . . .
My magic man, bring to my wheel the house I love . . .
My magic house, bring to my man the wheel I love . . .
My magic . . . my magic . . . my magic . . .'

E

Second Chorus Song

The Chorus of Aegean Voices

Voices of the early Aegean,
Glow, the smiling youth of a god.
Horseshoes kindle the cobbles,
In high voice, gulls, the harsh hawsers,
Boys with rough throats,
Agony of old hinges,
Light is born everywhere,
Agony and joy are born.

Voices of Aegean noon,
Wind lap in white wall,
Cicada, dry crackle,
There in the trees, there, lazy
Plain song behind the waterwheel,
From a tumbling porch by the sea,
Where men call to each other,
Heap maize in sacks
At the white point of noon.

Aegean voices of twilight.
Eyes of lovers speak in light,
Click of the wine-cup, sad hum of water
Spread through dust-green mulberries,
Spleen of the islands.
Wry women squat in the yards
Censed by honeysuckle,
Stitching gossip together.
They forget time and the gods,
And the dog's bark rubs
The outer edge of the ear.

Voices, Aegean night voices.
A silvery wind blows
Starlight into flame.
Cantillation of lovers
Threaded with salt air
Of silence, of moon-anointed
Silence, there, in the wind's pause,
There, the shivering jasmine
Flowers by the dripping wall.

F

Death of an Old Woman

Onlooker

She is lying alone, an old woman, alone
On her torn mattress.
Her eyes, like weary Argonauts,
Turning to stone. They are submissive,
Not cowardly eyes, submissive.
Anange, Anange . . .

—'Poetry, the study of the stars,
All arguments have taught me
That there is nothing more powerful than Anange.
Neither the Thracian tablets
With the charms, the recipes of Orpheus
Carved on stone,
Nor the herbs of Aesculapius,
Can give a cure.

She has no altar, no ancient statue,
No rite of persuasion.

All that Zeus, the Overlooker, allows
Is done through You . . .

Even the iron of the Chalybes you bend,
Steep and fearless Spirit . . .'

Nobody will really miss her.
There was a time when a streak of self-pity
Touched her heart—
When nobody will pity you,

You must pity yourself.
It was, when she first felt she had outlived
The hospitality of the body.
That did not last long.

There is a time for everything.
A time to be born, a time for rearing
Children, especially a time to say good-bye.
She had outlived even that.

Only the wind was faithful.
Blowing away the day she was born,
Blowing away the night her husband was drowned,
Blowing the morning her son left for the sea,
The deep song of her life,
The deep song of the island's life.
He was blowing again tonight,
When her eyes, like tired Argonauts,
Were turning to stone.
Anange, Necessity, Anange.
She had learnt to submit,
The greatest lesson, with dignity to submit.

How the wind was blowing,
Out of the womb of the sea!
Her eyes, not willing to remember,
Turned into stone, her hands drooping
Light, like the white leaves of an ancient tree
At night. But with that perfect dignity,
Dying, she was afraid.
Justice?

G

Onlooker

Every death is another approach.
With the old woman's death,
Under the cold green of water
The skull of the sunken city
Shifted in the sand.
A light gyrated upward,
With it a voice:

—'Do not remember me young. Remember me,
When the stone was no longer smooth,
When there was no more homecoming.
When the green foot of time
Had stamped a damp silence
On my temples, my streets,
My hands, the skeletons of ancient trees.
The young must learn to remember.'

Onlooker

Every death is a new approach.
The image increasingly shifts,
Less to be touched, more translucent.
Which is 'Home'?
Old and new fuse so fully in this
Grape-blue, tall Aegean light:
—'And my immortal body jumps in the wind.'